MAKING MAESTRO VISIBLE

Making Maestro Visible

Table Of Contents

Foreword

Making things of the mind give birth to something more tangible is one way of encouraging the individual to visualize and start working towards the thing that is being desired. Get everything you need to know about manifesting here.

Manifesting Maestro
Manifest Your Network Marketing Success

Chapter 1:

Manifesting Basics

Synopsis

For some people this manifesting element or thought process is something they have tried and swear by its positive contributions. The manifestation is apparent through the mental and physical realms and is very convincing to the individual convinced or its merits.

The Basics

This can be a very effective tool in training the mind to focus only on what the desired outcome should be in any given scenario and then concentrate on working towards effectively achieving that said preconceived idea.

This can be easily achieved if the individual is able to engage all his or her mind and body faculties to work as one energetically.

Making a choice to success at something is further cemented with the manifestation of that end picture to work towards.

Manifestations can effectively keep the individual centered and completely fixed on the end idea desired, thus ensuring distractions in any form don't cause the individual to lose this focus.

Manifestations are a conscious choice made by an individual and this tool can be explored to its optimum to ensure the product of the manifestation is achievable.

The manifestation exercise can help the individual pursuing a business venture to believe in its success and thus create the positive energy that will contribute to its eventual achievement.

Beliefs are just the thought process that is being constantly played out in the individual's mind.

Therefore positive manifestations will effectively equal positive beliefs which in turn will produce the desired positive results.

Chapter 2:

Decide On Your Specific Goal

Synopsis

It is easy to float around trying to achieve things without any specific direction in place. Unfortunately this aimless style does not contributed to phenomenal successes in any way which can be measured.

What Are You Going For

For most people who want to achieve something worthwhile, the goal setting exercise is something they take very seriously, as to them this is the first step towards the success platform of achievements.

Being specific about the goals to be set is definitely something to consider, as vaguely set goals will not yield the desired results and will only lead to confusion and even procrastination.

Specific goals will help the individual focus better on the way and means it is going to take to see these goals accomplished.

Creating a measurable platform where the processes contributing to the goal can be monitored is also another important element to design.

The measurable element will allow the monitoring process to be constant and will help to address any issues that need attention or redesigning. This will keep the goal achievement on track and within the time frame allotted.

Goals set should be attainable and within the realistic realm of the individual. Setting goals without these two considerations can cause adverse effects to the actual exercise or journey towards achieving the said goal.

Losing the initial excitement and momentum will further jeopardize the goal achieving exercise if the goals become more unattainable as reality sinks in.

Therefore it is very important to set smaller and less demanding goals that will help to create the confidence level to encourage the individual to aim for bigger goals at the next juncture.

Goals set also have to be done in a timely fashion. Rushing into goal setting without proper thought or complimenting tools and knowledge is also not advised.

Understanding that there is a time for everything is important to note otherwise the exercise will be defeated even before it begins.

Chapter 3:

Use Imagery

Synopsis

The human mind is a wonderful tool that should never be underestimated for its beneficial qualities when well tapped. Using the imagery method of getting people to commit or embark of something has proven to be effective over time.

Imagery is generally defined as a thought process where the sensory qualities of the mind will allow the individual to visualize something and translate this into probable other senses like hear, taste, smell, touch and feel.

Imagine

Using imagery to create the hunger in an individual when it comes to business ventures will help a great deal in the ensuring the individual is fully focused on the end goal that was designed at the onset of the business proposal or idea.

Being able to "plant" and image of phenomenal success that can be achieved with a particular endeavor will subconsciously keep the individual pushing towards the eventual reality of the reaching the desired goal.

The mental images formed will help the individual work towards that goal without succumbing towards any outside distractions.

Also by using imagery as a motivating tool the individual is able to actually "see and feel" the eventual outcome that he or she is working towards.

This is very powerful as working towards this type of goal is very exhilarating and energizing. There are very few instances where the imagery tools did not manifest the desired achievement of the goal set.

One of the reasons this may have happened is that the imagery set was unrealistic and thus unattainable. However this does not mean that all imagery used for goal setting should be done on a safe and boring tone but it simply means keeping some semblance of reality is necessary to ensuring the goal is attainable.

Integrating techniques that will positively contribute is also encouraged as some of these techniques produce surprisingly good results.

Chapter 4:

Synopsis

To understand the use of mantra with relation to the network marketing area one first has to understand the basis of mantra and its perceived capabilities. Mantras are sounds, syllables, words or groups of words that denotes the creating transference. This continuous transference will eventually be able to manifest itself into some reality through the actions both mentally and physically by the individual.

One Tool

Using mantras is very beneficial for the individual intending to embark on a business venture. For some the chanting of mantras helps them to stay focused and energized.

The almost mechanical repetitions of the mantra will subconsciously allow the individual to almost experience the possible positive outcome even before it has become a reality thereby keeping the individual constantly tuned into the success mode.

It has been documented that specific sounds emit stubble connective vibrations which in turn cause certain portions of the brain to come to a state of "awakening" to the idea behind the sound.

The collective emotional energy behind the words further enhance the already focused mind so that this added advantage can be expected to help overcome any possible setbacks that may arise through the course of the business foray.

There is also the positive effect the mantra has on the aura of the individual as it generally affects the energy shields surrounding the body.

The mantras will cause stubble changes in the emotions, intellect and soul and if used well it can keep the individual in the most optimum of conditions to carry out the business venture well and without any hiccups.

The sounds from the mantras can usually deeply influence the energy that is aligned to the individual.

Using the mantra to stay focused will also help to control the wandering s of the mind which is especially evident when there are distractions along the path to creating a successful business.

Chapter 5:

Use Affirmations

Synopsis

Creating a viable and successful networking platform comes with its own challenges and setbacks. Therefore having as many supporting tools as possible to help in any way is a definite plus.

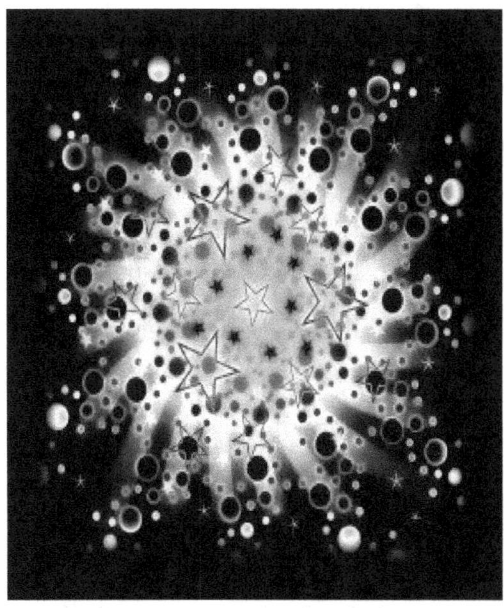

Believe It

The use of positive affirmation or positive pep self talks can not only benefit the individual itself but it can also benefit those around. The affirmation element allows the individual to shift all negative thoughts into the more beneficial positive platform and this in turn will yield better results, performance and attitudes.

Successful individuals have been known to consciously adopt this positive habit whereby they use a lot of positive words to bombard their mind and thought processes.

Rather than choosing to entertain negative elements or thoughts the affirmation use can reevaluate the situation to more it into a more dynamic and successful platform.

Affirmations can also contribute the individual's capabilities being exercised to reach its optimum. Elements such as strengths, talents, skills, can be encouraged to reach higher and more skilful platforms where there is the possibility of achieving things beyond originally anticipated.

An interesting fact to note is that affirmations come from the individual and is foremost in encouraging the dreams, ambitions, goals and other such future ideals into becoming a positive reality.

The right outlook, smiling demeanor, friendly approach among other things can and usually does contribute to the overall achievement standards of the endeavor. The will of an individual is the most powerful steering element that if nurtured well with the correct and beneficial affirmations is capable of keeping the individual on the road to success.

However knowing or defining what is desired or needed is the main ingredient towards being able to work on the right affirmations. The constant positive affirmations will serve and the fuel to the engine that brings the endeavor to its success.

Positive affirmations are powerful statements that should be adopted as often as possible in any circumstances.

Chapter 6:

Use Your Sleep Time For Manifesting

Synopsis

Being able to tap into all areas available to optimize results is something that everyone wants to be able to do. Therefore tapping into the sleep time to harness the positive elements it may manifest is just another avenue to explore. To fully understand and tap into the rather unknown area one must first understand the basics behind the sleep time manifesting idea.

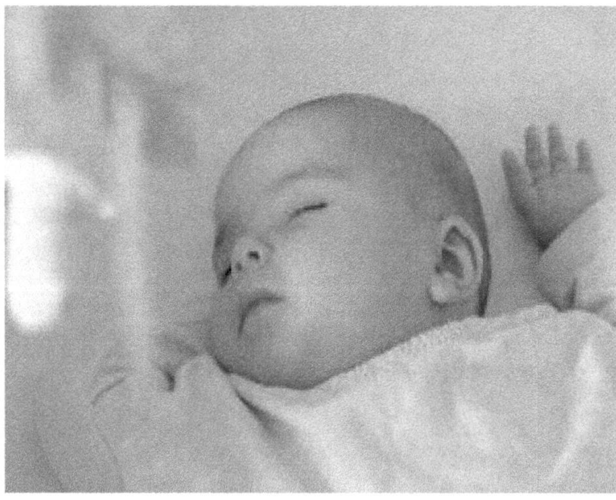

Your Dreams

The human mind is at work all the time, whether a person is awake or asleep. In sleep the subconscious mind will provide the necessary assistance to the organs of the body to continue functioning effectively.

When it come to the mind, most will find it difficult to quiet the mind in waking hours though if one is able to accomplish this feat there is a lot of positive value that can be derived from it.

The focus strengths of the mind are capable of this phenomena and this is what is going to benefit anyone who can channel this strength into physical demands in the business arena.

Being able to connect with higher thoughts and strengths is almost impossible in the day when the mind is so busy balancing different parts of its attention seeking platforms.

However during the sleep time sessions the mind is able to help the individual seeking answers and directions through communication with the higher inner self.

The inner self is focused only on the purity of helping with the best of intentions thus the relaxation mode can sufficiently provide for this pure state of mind. Naturally processing the matters that one is seeking some answers to will be better done during this time rather than stressing about it in the waking hours.

- 22 -

Allowing the body to relax and letting the mind search for the inner peace will eventually create the answers to questions most pressing.

Chapter 7:

Synopsis

Being energized, is probably the single most helpful phase to be constantly in, to ensure there is always some part of the individual that is tuned to opportunities available. Being able to be in the right place at the right time will definitely be a beneficial platform to work from but as that is not always possible the next best solution would be the connection to the surroundings that should be optimized.

The World

For most people the energy that is derived from being centered and connected to the universe is something they have grown accustomed to practicing and experiencing.

A lot of them will attest to the endless amount of energy that can be tapped into if the individual is open to the idea of connecting to the universe.

As most business endeavors move at a very fast and demanding pace, the need to stay energized will sometimes be a position of contention thus causing the individual to have to seek other means of staying energized.

Some of these maybe quite costly and cumbersome to practice, therefore connecting to the energy available from the surrounding or the universe can help to make the quest easier and less stressful.

There are several techniques available today to help those interested to tap into the realm of connecting with the universe. It would be beneficial for the individual to find one that is most useful and easy to follow and then practice harnessing this energy as a daily routine.

Using the energy from the connection to the universe one should also strive to be the best in the chosen area and this can be done with guidance and perseverance. Working with some level of purpose and being sure that one in contributing positively to society at large will make the connection to the universe even more meaningful.

Chapter 8:

Synopsis

Life in general becomes much more manageable if one has the unshakeable ability to believe in oneself. This quality is one that is worth developing especially if there is the need to make a success of any business venture currently underway.

You Can Do It

Upon discovering or realizing one's purpose in life or simply upon discovering an ideal business opportunity that presents itself the ideal and recommended next step to take would be to write down and place the written idea in a visible and attention grabbing position to ensure that the material is constantly being viewed and thus being kept foremost in the individual's mind.

The more visible the material the more the individual is going to be bombarded with its content. Eventually the individual will be able to accept the idea as a "given" and work on the idea as if it has already achieved success.

The quality of being able to believe in the endeavor at hand and the capabilities of those involved does take some getting used to but if done in an encouraging manner there is very little room for doubts to be created.

However this does not translate to mean that all things will become easier and smooth flowing once the belief element has been established. It simply means that one will now be equipped with the positive mindset that will be able to adequate combat any possible adversities.

There are many reasons why one should actively develop this mindset and the following are just some to ponder upon:

- When the ability to believe is evident, the individual can usually easily change or work on negative situations to be turned into more positive and manageable ones.

- Wanting to accomplish different things and face challenging situations also requires some level of belief to be developed. Most people who believe in themselves are programmed to act as if they are capable of accomplishing almost anything and when the mind of sure of this the body generally follows suit.

Wrapping Up

Manifestation is the creation and control of one own experiences. Through the manifestation exercise the individual is able to manipulate elements that are not pleasing and substitute these with more desired elements according to their own perceptions.

Start using it today.

www.ingramcontent.com/pod-product-compliance
Lightning Source LLC
LaVergne TN
LVHW050305200726
843509LV00015B/3161